WO
WF

Paul Stickland

Dutton   LODESTAR   New York

A moving van takes furniture to a new home.

The ambulance will carry the man on the stretcher to the hospital.

The street sweeper cleans the street.

The cement mixer pours concrete.

The fire truck has a platform that can be raised or lowered.

These workers are building a new road and using the roller to make it smooth.

The sanitation workers are emptying
garbage into the garbage truck.